EXPANDED EDITION
Grade 2

The **Build It!** lesson is part of the Picture-Perfect STEM program K–2 written by the program authors and includes lessons from their award-winning series.

Additional information about using the Picture Perfect Science series, including key reading strategies, NGSS connections, and the BSCS 5E instructional model can be downloaded for free at:

Build It!

Description

Children love to build. In this lesson, they use their creativity to build structures out of everyday materials. Next, they are introduced to a variety of iconic buildings and learn about the architects who designed them. Finally, students design and build architectural models of some of these famous structures.

Alignment with the *Next Generation Science Standards*

Performance Expectation		
2-PS1-3: Make observations to construct an evidence-based account of how an object made of a small set of pieces can be disassembled and made into a new object.		
Science and Engineering Practice	**Disciplinary Core Idea**	**Crosscutting Concept**
Developing and Using Models Develop a simple model based on evidence to represent a proposed object or tool.	**PS1.A: Structure and Properties of Matter** A great variety of objects can be built up from a small set of pieces.	**Scale, Proportion, and Quantity** Relative scales allow objects and events to be compared and described (e.g., bigger and smaller, hotter and colder, faster and slower).

Note: The activities in this lesson will help students move toward the performance expectation listed, which is the goal after multiple activities. However, the activities will not by themselves be sufficient to reach the performance expectation.

Featured Picture Books

TITLE: **Iggy Peck, Architect**
AUTHOR: **Andrea Beaty**
ILLUSTRATOR: **David Roberts**
PUBLISHER: **Abrams Books for Young Readers**
YEAR: **2007**
GENRE: **Story**
SUMMARY: *Iggy Peck spends every waking hour building things, until second grade, when his teacher forbids it. He finally wins her over by using his skills to save the day on his class field trip.*

TITLE: **Dreaming Up: A Celebration of Building**
AUTHOR: **Christy Hale**
ILLUSTRATOR: **Christy Hale**
PUBLISHER: **Lee & Low Books**
YEAR: **2012**
GENRE: **Non-Narrative Information**
SUMMARY: *This book is a unique celebration of children's playtime explorations and the surprising ways childhood experiences find expression in the dreams and works of innovative architects. Each spread features illustrations of children building various structures as they play, paired with a photograph of an actual building that uses the same basic ideas and principles. Information on each featured building and its architect is contained in the end matter.*

Time Needed

This lesson will take several class periods. Suggested scheduling is as follows:

Session 1: Engage with *Iggy Peck, Architect* Read-Aloud and **Explore** with Free Build

Session 2: Explain with *Dreaming Up* Read-Aloud and Famous Buildings and Structures Video

Session 3: Elaborate with Iggy's Models and Architecture Journal

Session 4 and beyond: Evaluate with Build It! and Architecture Expo

Materials

For Free Build (per group of 3–6 students)

Each group receives a different set of building materials modeled after the book *Dreaming Up*, such as

- **Group 1:** Small paper or plastic cups and masking tape
- **Group 2:** Empty tissue or other small boxes and masking tape
- **Group 3:** Playing cards and painter's tape
- **Group 4:** Toothpicks and packing peanuts
- **Group 5:** Cardboard tubes, brown paper grocery or lunch bags, masking tape, and scissors
- **Group 6:** Craft sticks and masking tape

For Iggy's Models

- Images of the Gateway Arch, Golden Gate Bridge, Great Sphinx of Giza, Hōryū-ji temple, Leaning Tower of Pisa, and Neuschwanstein Castle

For Build It!

- Bins of the supplies used in the Free Build activity
- Pencils, crayons, and markers

Student Pages

- Architecture Journal
- STEM Everywhere

Background for Teachers

In this lesson, students are introduced to the fascinating world of architecture, a discipline that combines science, engineering, and art in the design of buildings. A Roman architect and engineer named Vitruvius, who lived in the first century BC, asserted that there were three principles of good architecture:

- **Durability**: Structures should be made of the right materials to stand up, be safe, and remain in good condition.
- **Utility**: Structures should be useful and function well for the people using them.
- **Beauty**: Structures should delight people and raise their spirits.

Although these principles originated thousands of years ago, they still hold true today. To achieve these goals, architects plan the overall appearance of buildings, while ensuring that they are safe, functional, and economical. Sketches, plans, elevation drawings, and architectural models are important tools in communicating an architect's ideas.

The *Framework* suggests that students in grades K–12 are engaged in the science and engineering practice (SEP) of developing and using models. In the early grades, these models progress from making diagrams and replicas to developing models to represent a new object or tool. This lesson uses models in the context of architecture. The lesson begins with a "free build" activity in which students work with building materials, such as cups, craft sticks, boxes, and cardboard tubes to create something new. Young children need time to tinker with a variety of materials to develop their understanding of how small pieces can be assembled into objects and structures and how objects and structures can be disassembled into smaller pieces.

Next, students are exposed to some iconic buildings from a range of historical periods, learn about famous architects and their inspirations, and reuse some of the materials they worked with during the explore phase to create sketches and design architectural models of buildings. Building models encourages children to test spatial relationships and mentally rotate objects, which can help them to develop better spatial abilities. It is important to note that models are not always physical. They can also be mental or conceptual. "Modeling can begin in the earliest grades, with students' models progressing from concrete 'pictures' and/or physical scale models to more abstract representations of relevant relationships in later grades, such as a diagram representing forces on a particular object or system" (Willard, 2015 p. 7). An architectural model is a type of scale model—a physical representation of a structure—that

is used to study aspects of architectural design or to communicate design ideas. Architects construct these models using a variety of materials, including blocks, paper, and wood, just as students do in the elaborate phase of the lesson. This activity provides opportunities for students to create drawings and physical models just as real architects do.

The crosscutting concept (CCC) of structure and function is highlighted throughout the lesson as students learn how the shape and stability of a structure, such as a building, bridge, or skyscraper, is related to its function.

Learning Progressions

Below are the disciplinary core idea (DCI) grade band endpoints for grades K–2 and 3–5. These are provided to show how student understanding of the DCIs in this lesson will progress in future grade levels.

DCI	Grades K–2	Grades 3–5
PS1.A: Matter and Its Interactions	• A great variety of objects can be built up from a small set of pieces.	• Measurements of a variety of properties can be used to identify materials.

Source: Willard, T., ed. 2015. *The NSTA quick-reference guide to the* NGSS: *Elementary school.* Arlington, VA: NSTA Press.

engage

Iggy Peck, Architect Read-Aloud

**Inferring**

Show students the cover of *Iggy Peck, Architect* and introduce the author, Andrea Beaty, and the illustrator, David Roberts. *Ask*

? From looking at the cover and title, what do you think this book is about? (Answers will vary.)

? What do you think an architect does? (Students may know that architects are involved in designing buildings.)

**Questioning**

Read the book aloud. Then *ask*

? What kinds of materials did Iggy Peck use to build the structures in the book? (chalk, pancakes, apples, dirt, etc.)

? How did Iggy's teacher feel about his passion for building? (She did not like it.) What evidence from the text makes you think that? (She would not allow him to build at school.)

? What happened to his teacher that made her dislike architecture? (She got lost on an architect's tour and was stuck in an elevator with a French circus troupe.)

? How did Iggy finally win his teacher over? (He used his building expertise to build a bridge to rescue the class.)

Making Connections: Text to Self

Ask

? Do you like to build things like the character Iggy Peck? (Answers will vary.)

? What materials have you used to build something? (Have students share with a partner.)

Tell students that the author, Andrea Beaty, was inspired to write this book because her son had a passion for building when he was young. He would build with anything he could get his hands on. He built towers out of soup cans from their pantry and houses out of jelly packets at restaurants.

 explore

Free Build

Tell students that they are going to have the opportunity to be like Iggy Peck and use their imaginations and some everyday materials to create a structure. Divide students into groups of three to six, and explain that each group will receive different supplies for building. Each student will build his or her own structure, but the group will share the supplies. Afterward, students will have a chance to share their structures. Give each group a container with the supplies listed in the "Materials" section (p. 192). Set a time limit and let them build!

> **CCC: Scale, Proportion, and Quantity**
> Relative scales allow objects to be compared and described (e.g., bigger and smaller).

When students are finished, have them clean up their supplies and display their structures on their tables or desks. Invite students within each group to compare their structures. Pose the follow-

FREE BUILD

ing questions to move students' thinking toward the idea that although they all had the same set of pieces to work with, all of their structures were very different. *Ask*

? In your group, what shapes were the building materials?

? What shapes could you put together to make other shapes?

? How are your group's structures the same?

? How are they different?

? Which structure in your group is the tallest? Widest?

? Which uses the most materials?

? Which uses the least materials?

Point out that there was no right or wrong way to build these structures. Each person used their imagination and had a different vision for how to build the structures. A great variety of objects can be built from a small set of pieces.

You may want to set up an area to display each structure or take photographs of each one and hang them in the classroom to create a class display. You can refer to this display during the activities in the explain phase of the lesson.

explain

Dreaming Up Read-Aloud

Determining Importance

Show students the cover of *Dreaming Up: A Celebration of Building* and introduce Christy Hale, the author and illustrator of this book. Tell students that the supplies that were used in the free build activity were all inspired by this book. As you read the book aloud, have students signal (touch their noses) when you come to a two-page spread where the illustration on the left-hand page shows the supplies they used to build their structures. Compare the structures in the illustrations with the structures students made. Explain that these different structures are examples of how a great variety of objects can be made from a small set of pieces.

> ### Connecting to the Common Core
> **Mathematics**
> KEY IDEAS AND DETAILS: 2.7

Then compare each illustrated structure with the photograph of the actual building on the right-hand page. Have students notice similarities in lines and shapes among the structures the children built and the lines and shapes found in the actual buildings. Some examples are as follows:

COMPARING STRUCTURES

- Pages 3–4: The cups have a nearly cylindrical shape similar to the Petronas Towers.
- Pages 7–8: The box has a rectangular prism shape similar to the Box House.
- Pages 17–18: The playing cards are thin and straight, which is similar to the linear shapes on the Vitra Fire Station.
- Pages 19–20: The toothpicks and gumdrops form small triangles similar to the triangles that make up the large sphere of the Montreal Biosphere.
- Pages 25–26: The paper towel tubes are cylinders similar to the cylinders supporting the roofs and walls of the Paper Tube School.
- Pages 27–28: The shape of the craft sticks is similar to the wooden planks that make up the cylinder shape of Sclera Pavilion.

Next, *ask*

? Do you notice any patterns in this book? (Students may notice that on the left-hand side of each page is an illustration of kids building, and on the right-hand side is a photograph of an actual building. They may also notice that the way the text is arranged on the page is similar to the structures pictured.)

As an example, share pages 13–14, which show children building a sandcastle on the left-hand page and a photograph of La Sagrada Família on the right-hand page. Explain to students that Hale's poem compares children's building experiences (page 13) to real buildings (page 14).

Synthesizing

Then *ask*

? Why do you think the author of this book compared this famous building, La Sagrada Família, to a sandcastle? (It is the same color as sand and the same shape.)

? Why do you think the author and illustrator of this book, Christy Hale, decided to create the book this way? (Answers will vary.)

Features of Nonfiction

Connecting to the Common Core
Reading: Informational Text
CRAFT AND STRUCTURE: 2.5

Model how to find information about the author by looking at the back flap of the book jacket. Read the section that explains Hale's vision for this book:

> *Her inspiration for* Dreaming Up *dates back to her first encounter with Barcelona's La Sagrada Família. "I'm sure I made the sandcastle connection way back then," says Hale. From then on, "it became a fun challenge to think of the many ways kids build, and then buildings that correspond to their building play."*

Explain that this cathedral, La Sagrada Família, was Hale's first inspiration for this book. After seeing how it resembled a child's sandcastle, she started to notice how other structures resembled things that children build.

Connecting to the Common Core
Reading: Informational Text
CRAFT AND STRUCTURE: 2.7

Questioning

Explain that the very different buildings featured in this book were designed by different architects. Show students the last four pages that discuss the architects for each building. Read a few of the sections aloud. You may want to begin with Cesar Pelli and the Petronas Towers. *Ask*

? Why do you think Cesar Pelli used this shape (tapered like graduated cups) for the Petronas Towers? (Being wider at the bottom gives them more stability so they can reach higher.)

? Why do you think Pelli used concrete, steel, and glass to make the Petronas Towers? (Concrete and steel are strong; glass is lighter and lets light in.)

Allow students to suggest some other architects for you to read aloud about. After each one, go back to the page that shows the building that architect designed and *ask*

? Why do you think this architect used this shape for this structure? (Answers will vary but should reflect that the shape is related to the building's purpose or function.)

? What materials did the architect use on the building in the book? Why do you think they used those materials? (Answers will vary but should include that the materials are related to the stability and durability of the building as well as the overall shape.)

After reading about several architects, *ask*

? How are these architects different? (Some are men and some are women. They are different ethnicities, ages, and backgrounds. They have different inspirations. They designed with different materials and for different purposes.)

? What do all of these architects have in common? (They liked to build when they were young. They are creative.)

Synthesizing
Ask

? After reading both *Iggy Peck, Architect* and *Dreaming Up*, how have your ideas changed about what an architect does?

Famous Buildings and Structures Video

 *Making Connections: Text to Text*

Tell students that you have a video to show them called "100 Most Famous Buildings/Structures of All Time" (see "Websites"). Explain that these particular buildings were chosen by the video's creator and that other people might have other ideas about the world's most famous buildings. Tell them that the video is set to music from the era, or historical time period, of each set of buildings. As you watch, have students signal when they see a building they recognize. It could be a building from *Dreaming Up*, a building they have visited, or a building they have seen in other books or videos. (Many students will likely recognize the Taj Mahal, Leaning Tower of Pisa, Eiffel Tower, and Gateway Arch.) After viewing, *ask*

? What buildings did you recognize from the book *Dreaming Up*? (Fallingwater, Habitat 67, Petronas Towers, Guggenheim Museum, and La Sagrada Família are all pictured.)

? What information was given for each building shown? (name, architect, and year built)

? What building materials did you recognize in the video? (stone, metal, concrete, etc.)

? Do you think those materials were the right choices for durability? (Yes, because all of these buildings are still standing.)

? Do all of the buildings look the same? (no)

? Why do you think the buildings look different? (They serve different purposes and were designed by different architects.)

? What are some of the uses for the different buildings in the video? (homes, churches, monuments, office buildings, etc.)

? Which buildings did you like the most? (Answers will vary.)

? Do you think that all of the buildings are beautiful? (Answers will vary.)

Explain that "beauty is in the eye of the beholder." Some people may criticize an architect's building, whereas other people may think the same building is very beautiful!

elaborate

Iggy's Models

Connecting to the Common Core
Reading: Informational Text
CRAFT AND STRUCTURE: 2.1

Revisit the book *Iggy Peck, Architect* and flip through the illustrations. Point out to students that Iggy is not just building random things in the book. He is actually creating models of famous buildings (some of which were in the video they just watched!). So, Iggy not only likes to build but also likes to study architecture.

Search online for photographs of famous buildings referenced in the book and have students compare Iggy's model with the actual building:

• Page 4: He uses diapers to create a model of the Leaning Tower of Pisa.

• Page 7: He uses dirt clods to make a model of the Great Sphinx of Giza.

• Pages 8–9: He uses modeling clay and pencils to make a model of Hōryū-ji temple.

• Pages 10–11: He uses pancakes and pie to make a model of the Gateway Arch.

• Page 18: He uses chalk to build a model of Neuschwanstein Castle.

• Pages 28–29: The bridge he builds is modeled after the Golden Gate Bridge.

Architecture Journal

Connecting to the Common Core
Writing
TEXT TYPES AND PURPOSES: 2.2

 *Writing*

Give each student a copy of the Architecture Journal student pages. Tell students that they are going to have another opportunity to build something. However, unlike the first time, when their challenge was just to build something creative out of the materials they were given, this time they are going to build a model of an actual building. They will complete all the pages in the journal first, and then they will design and build a model of the building they chose.

> **SEP: Developing and Using Models**
> Develop a simple model based on evidence to represent a proposed object.

Architecture Journal Pages:

- Cover: Students write their name and decorate the journal cover any way they like.

- Pages 1–2: Students glue or tape pictures of some buildings they like. They can cut the pictures out of magazines or print them from images found online (search "famous buildings").

- Page 3: Students select the building they want to model and tape or glue a photo here. They also label the shapes they recognize in the building.

- Page 4: Students research some information about the building: the name, architect, location, and the materials used in the building.

- Page 5: Students think carefully about which materials would be best to represent their building and then circle the materials they plan to use to make their model.

- Page 6: Students sketch a plan of how they will use those materials to make a model of the building they chose.

evaluate

Build It!

As students are working on their journals, review their sketches and provide feedback on their choice of materials for their models. *Ask*

? Why did you choose that building?

? Why did you choose those materials?

Next, they can build their model! Provide all of the building supplies from the Free Build activity (explore phase) in bins for students to access as they build. Encourage students to look closely at the photograph of their building. They may also use pencils, crayons, and markers to add details to their models.

Architecture Expo

Tell students that they are going to get to share their models with a visiting class at an architecture expo. Have students display their models on their desks. They should have their Architecture Journal open to pages 3–4 so that visitors can see a photograph of the building, its name, the architect, location, and materials used to build it. Have students do a gallery walk through the classroom, using sticky notes to post suggestions, questions, and positive feedback on the desks next to the models. Writing on sticky notes encourages interaction, and the comments provide immediate feedback for the "exhibitors."

A few guidelines for a gallery walk are as follows:

- All necessary information about the model should be provided in the display (pages 3–4 of the Architecture Journal) because students will not be giving an oral presentation.

- Like a visit to an art gallery, the gallery walk should be done quietly. Students should be respectful of the displays. You may even want to play soft, classical music to set the tone.

STEM Everywhere

Give students the STEM Everywhere student page as a way to involve their families and extend their learning. They can do the activity with an adult helper and share their results with the class. If students do not have access the internet at home, you may choose to have them complete this activity at school.

Opportunities for Differentiated Instruction

This box lists questions and challenges related to the lesson that students may select to research, investigate, or innovate. Students may also use the questions as examples to help them generate their own questions. These questions can help you move your students from the teacher-directed investigation to engaging in the science and engineering practices in a more student-directed format.

Extra Support

For students who are struggling to meet the lesson objectives, provide a question and guide them in the process of collecting research or helping them design procedures or solutions.

Extensions

For students with high interest or who have already met the lesson objectives, have them choose a question (or pose their own question), conduct their own research, and design their own procedures or solutions.

After selecting one of the questions in the box or formulating their own question, students can individually or collaboratively make predictions, design investigations or surveys to test their predictions, collect evidence, devise explanations, design solutions, or examine related resources. They can communicate their findings through a science notebook, at a poster session or gallery walk, or by producing a media project.

Research

Have students brainstorm researchable questions:

? What are the tallest buildings in the world, and who designed them?

? Who designed your school, and what year was it built?

? What materials were used to build your school, and why did the builder choose those materials?

Continued

Opportunities for Differentiated Instruction (continued)

Investigate

Have students brainstorm testable questions to be solved through science or math:

? What materials can hold the most weight without breaking: rubber bands, paper strips, or toothpicks?

? What materials could be used to make a model of a geodesic dome?

? Which shape can support the most weight: a triangular prism, a rectangular prism, or a cylinder?

Innovate

Have students brainstorm problems to be solved through engineering:

? What structure could you design for your school playground?

? What structure could you design to represent your school spirit?

? What would your dream house look like? What features would it have and what materials would you use?

Websites

 "100 Most Famous Buildings/Structures of All Time"(video)
www.youtube.com/ watch?v=dA3Ak-FLk_A

 PBS: Style in Architecture (video) www.pbs.org/video/ artquest-style-architecture

More Books to Read

Ames, L. 2013. *Draw 50 buildings and other structures: The step-by-step way to draw castles and cathedrals, skyscrapers and bridges, and so much more …* New York: Watson-Guptill.
Summary: This step-by-step book filled with black-and-white line drawings reduces famous buildings such as the Taj Mahal and the Eiffel Tower (and other buildings such as igloos and castles) to basic lines and shapes. It then shows young artists how to put the shapes together and add details to represent each building.

Guarnaccia, S. 2010. *The three little pigs: An architectural tale*. New York: Abrams Books for Young Readers.
Summary: In this quirky retelling of the three little pigs, the pigs and their homes are nods to three famous architects—Frank Gehry, Philip Johnson, and Frank Lloyd Wright—and their signature homes. Each house is filled with clever details, including furnishing by the architects and their contemporaries. Of course, not all the houses are going to protect the pigs from the wolf's huffing and puffing. The wolf, and readers, are in for a clever surprise ending.

Harvey, J. 2017. *Maya Lin: Artist-architect of light and lines*. New York: Henry Holt and Company.
Summary: Elegant, simple writing paired with Dow Phumiruk's crisp, clean-lined illustrations tell the story of the inspiring American artist and architect who designed the Vietnam Veterans Memorial.

Hayden, K. 2003. *Amazing buildings*. New York: DK Children.
Summary: Simple text and vivid photographs depict how some of the world's most famous buildings were made.

Lyons, K. 2020. *Dream builder: The story of architect Phillip Freelon*. New York: Lee & Low Books.
Summary: This picture book biography celebrates a contemporary STEAM role model, an architect who overcame early struggles with reading to become a designer of schools, libraries, and museums that honor Black heritage and culture.

Ritchie, S. 2011. *Look at that building!: A first book of structures*. Tonawanda, NY: Kids Can Press.
Summary: Come along as the five friends from *Follow That Map!* start a whole new adventure. Max the dog needs a new doghouse to live in, so the gang is on a quest to find out all it can about buildings and how they are constructed.

Roeder, A. 2011. *13 buildings children should know*. New York: Prestel Verlag.
Summary: From the Great Pyramid of Giza to the Beijing National Stadium, this book presents 13 famous buildings from around the world. It includes information about the architect, location, materials, and special features of each building.

Stevenson, R. L. 2005. *Block city*. New York: Simon & Schuster Books for Young Readers.
Summary: This illustrated version of Robert Louis Stevenson's classic poem also includes folk songs, building projects, and math activities.

Van Dusen, C. 2019. *If I built a school*. New York: Dial Books
Summary: Chris Van Dusen's trademark rhymes and imaginative illustrations describe young Jack's dream school, including hover desks, skydiving wind tunnels, and a trampoline basketball court.

Winter, J. 2017. *The world is not a rectangle: A portrait of architect Zaha Hadid*. San Diego, CA: Beach Lane Books.
Summary: This picture book biography of famed Iraqi architect Zaha Hadid, known for her unconventional building design, describes the obstacles she had to overcome as well as the tremendous success she enjoyed throughout her career.

Architecture Journal

Name: _____

Buildings I Like

Tape or glue some photographs of buildings you like.

- -

Sketch

What will your model look like if you build it using only those materials? Make a sketch.

page 2

Materials

Playing Cards

Craft sticks

Boxes

Tubes

Toothpicks

Paper bags

Cups

Index cards

Packing peanuts

Other (draw):

page 5

Photo

Tape or glue a photograph of the building you want to model. Label the shapes you see in the building.

Research

Record some details about the building.

Name of Building:

_____

Architect:

_____

Location:

_____

This building is used for:

_____

_____

This building is constructed of these materials:

_____

_____

Name: _____

STEM Everywhere

At school, we have been learning about **how architects use different shapes and materials in their designs and that the shape of a building relates to the purpose of the building**. To find out more, ask your learner questions such as:

- What did you learn?
- What was your favorite part of the lesson?
- What are you still wondering?

 At home, watch a short video titled "Artquest: Style In Architecture" exploring different styles of architecture. *www.pbs.org/video/ artquest-style-architecture*

After you watch the video, look for the shapes that make up a building in your neighborhood.

Sketch of Building	Label the Shapes You Found
	Triangle Square Circle
	Arc Rectangle Cylinder